THROUGH THE SMOKER

WHAT BBQ CAN TEACH YOU ABOUT HOW GOD PREPARES A MAN

WESLEY PENNINGTON

urbanpress

TESTIMONIALS

Wes is a sterling example of a man of unimpeachable character and unassailable integrity. I have watched this modern day Phoenix rise to be the personification of a man of integrity, committed to empowering men to be the same. When I think of men who have left an indelible mark in my life, Wes Pennington tops the list. If you're looking for an inspiring and empowering messenger, Wes is your guy.
– Jeffery A. Williams, D. Min., MPA
President/Chief Empowerment Strategist,
The Williams Empowerment Group, LLC

Whether it's on the football field or behind the pulpit, Wes has a sincerity to his call that is unparalleled. He is a leader of men, even in the arena of great men. His delivery has a level of caring and compassion that causes others to want to be better. One of the words that personally comes to mind when I think of Wes is integrity and I am so very proud to call him brother and friend.
– Elder Donovan C. Woodruff

Rev. Wesley Pennington is a bona-fide coach who draws out the best in male audiences of all demographics. His life-experience of being a war hero in the United States Military, a celebrated Rhode Island State Police sergeant for 26 years and a men's pastor positions him uniquely as a speaker that captures the attention of most men. He speaks with light-hearted humor, practical wisdom, and depth of biblical understanding but most notably, his passionate love for Jesus and His sheep. Without question, your group, church, men's ministry, or anyone else who hears him will be all the better after they hear Wes speak.
– Dr. Michael Caparrelli,
Wes's pastor for ten years

Through the Smoker
by Wesley Pennington
Copyright ©2021 Wesley Pennington

ISBN 978-1-63360-183-3

For Worldwide Distribution
Printed in the USA

Urban Press
P.O. Box 8881
Pittsburgh, PA 15221-0881
412.646.2780

CONTENTS

FOREWORD

It's not often I come across a new book that both inspires and challenges me while at the same time shedding light on how life works. I have had the honor of knowing Wes Pennington for 15 years as a colleague in ministry, public servant, husband, and father. I've witnessed his remarkable transformation he shares with you in the pages that follow.

The book you hold in your hands is a tried-and-true collection of lessons that comprise an effective manual for personal growth. Each page contains real-life success strategies that will help you sidestep unnecessary failures. *Through the Smoker* is not only relevant to the needs of our present culture, but clearly speaks to the heart of both boys and men alike.

The Bible describes God's process, indicating that everything develops in stages. Wes captures the essence of process and deftly connects the culinary art form of smoking meats with the maturing process from boyhood to manhood. It's a joy to see how he describes his personal growth and journey and then effortlessly and accurately applies it to the essence of every man's journey.

As the old adage goes, "When the student is ready, the teacher appears." Well, the teacher is Wes and school is in session through this manual for maturation. The only question that remains is: Are you ready?

Bishop Jeffery A. Williams, D. Min, MPA

ACKNOWLEDGMENTS

I would like to take a moment to thank several people who have been instrumental in my being able to write this book. First and foremost, I would like to thank my Lord Jesus Christ to whom goes all the glory for calling me to this purpose.

As is often said, behind every great man is a greater woman. I would like to thank my beautiful wife, Marissa, for putting up with my long hours of study in the process of writing this book. Marissa, I would not be the man I am today if you had not come into my life.

Next, I would like to thank my beautiful daughter, Ashley, for helping me with my website and making her dad look good.

I would like to say thank you to one of my best friends, mentors, and pastor, Dr. Mike Caparrelli. It's true what they say about talent. If you want to be great, be around those who are great. Being around you Pastor Mike (as I call him) has made me a better person. Like I said to you a few years ago, God gave you the seeds for my future. Thank you for planting them in good soil.

I would also like to thank Dr. Jeffery A. Williams who wrote the foreword for this book. You challenge me to go higher and know my why.

By watching you, I can see the road to greatness through faith. You are a vital part of this journey I am on, and I thank God for sending a strong warrior to go through this process with.

I would also like to thank Pastor Frank Reedy, my senior pastor, for allowing me the room to grow. You gave me freedom to grow and learn and you have taught me how to really understand Scripture. Thank you.

A special thank you goes to Dr. Delatorro L. McNeal who gave me the idea of combining my BBQ techniques with the process of manhood. Thank you, Delatorro, for opening my mind to the blessings of God that are not thought of as spiritual. You have challenged me to step out of the traditional thought of ministry in order the reach a broad population of men.

I would like to thank the Rally Point Men's Ministry board of directors. Thank you, my mighty brothers, for walking arm-in-arm with me in our objective of awakening and bringing the tribes together. We have much work ahead of us to do.

Finally, I would like to thank you for reading this book. I hope that you are now able to understand your personal God process in a different way. It has been through my love of BBQ that God has shown me the unique way He brings men through the process of maturity and personal growth. We all must go through the smoker.

When you are in it, know that you're not alone. You have the entire body of Christ in there with you. What's more, the Lord your God is in there with you as well. If we remember, in the story of Shadrach, Meshach, and Abednego, they were thrown into a fiery furnace. However, when Nebuchadnezzar looked in, he did not see three men but four walking around in the fire. That's because God does not just put us through the smoker; He is standing in there with us. Bless you and may you bless the next man with a copy of this book.

INTRODUCTION

This book is not a biography, but it's important for you to know where I am coming from and how I got to where I am today. Let's go back to the very beginning. I grew up in a house with five boys and one girl, and I am the fifth boy of the five. My mother had us all in church every Sunday and consequently, I've had a strong faith in God since I was a young boy. I can remember praying to God for things for which little boys usually pray, things like girlfriends and lots of success on the football field. Yet despite these childish expressions, I realized early in life that my faith was an important part of who I am.

Even though I could not see it back then, now I know God was present in my life all along. Like Jacob, the Lord was in my life but "I knew it not." I remember one day when my older brother Alex came to me and asked if I had some money. I instantly reached into my pocket and gave him my only quarter, saying, "This is all I have," but I still gave it to him. Later that day I was riding my bike to go see a friend.

As I got to the corner of the road, I was going to turn right when something in the middle of the road caught my eye. This was Route 6, a very busy road, but I put my bike down, looked both ways, and was surprised that not one car was coming in either direction. I walked out to the middle of the street and lo and behold, I found a quarter. Then I saw another quarter, and another. I stood in the middle of Route 6 picking up quarter after quarter until I had recovered eight dollars in quarters from the middle of the road—all without a single car appearing to interrupt my harvest.

I didn't realize it then, but God had orchestrated the circumstances for me to find and retrieve those quarters after I had given my only quarter away. That story is indicative of my entire life. Throughout this book, I will share more stories of my childhood and adulthood to help explain my position on manhood so you can see it from my point of view.

I played football in high school and in college. I even played some semi-pro football and now I am the head coach for a high school football team in West Warwick, Rhode Island. I served in the Army full-time for four years, am a war veteran, and served four years in the National Guard. As a soldier, I was assigned to the 82nd Airborne Division when the first Gulf War started. I had just come from Korea after a year there on a hardship tour and then was assigned to Fort Bragg, so I came home, picked up my family, and drove to North Carolina. Within a week of arriving at Fort Bragg, I was shipped off to Saudi Arabia just two days after the invasion of Kuwait. I spent nine months in the desert enduring 120-degree weather. While I was there, I received a revelation which has carried me through my 27-year career in law enforcement.

As you can imagine, going off to war is frightening. I wondered if I would make it home again to see my family and friends. One day as I was praying, I felt the Spirit ask if God was in charge of when and how I died. My answer was that He is. Then I was asked the question, "Does it matter if you're home in bed nice and comfortable or here in the desert?" I said it didn't matter for when it's time to go home, it's time.

Then I felt the Spirit say, "Then don't worry." From that point on and for the past 27 years as a state trooper, that revelation has carried me through some hair-raising encounters—but I digress. Upon completion of my military obligations, I became a police officer, having wanted to be a state trooper since I was a child. When I was six years old, I was traveling with my father and mother and little sister to visit family in Connecticut when my father got stopped by a state trooper.

I was sitting in the back seat looking out the back window when I saw the trooper step out of his police car. He had his sunglasses on and as he was getting out, he put on his Stetson hat. I could have sworn when the sun hit his cross strap buckle and reflected such a brilliant light that if it could have made a sound, it would have sounded like "ting." I watched him all the way to the door of my father's car. I don't remember if my father got a ticket or not but from that point on, all I wanted to do was be a state trooper. I had no plan B.

Back home after the Army, I applied to be a state trooper.

As I write this, I am a 27-year veteran of the Rhode Island State Police. I have reached the rank of sergeant and as I approach my imminent retirement in 2022, I look back and realize those 27 years have gone by quickly. I give you all this background because I know what manhood and masculinity looks, acts, and feels like. I have been groomed in the art of manhood through my experiences in life. I want to share what I have learned with you because I feel we have lost our masculinity in our country and probably all over the world. Let me explain what I mean and why I make that claim.

What is the difference between masculinity and femininity? We all have the traits of both in us at the same time. A man must be able to get in touch with his femininity without losing his masculinity to be effective. This sounds difficult and maybe even confusing, but it's as simple as showing compassion for someone who is sick or giving mercy to those who need it.

Masculine and feminine energy run together in both sexes. We even observe this in same sex couples. One partner usually has the more feminine side while the other has the more masculine side, even though they are both the same sex. This again indicates that we have both energies or traits in us. It's just that men usually don't want to show their side that is more closely associated with femininity.

I have produced teaching material to help

men become better men called the *Pennington Power Process* and will include some of that material in this book. I will walk you through some attitudes or principles that men must recognize, heed, and act upon. Paul wrote that when we were children, we acted and thought like children. When we matured and became men, we were supposed to put childish things behind us. Therefore, men need to start putting childish things behind them. Our Lord and Savior never acted like a child. He was focused on His mission but said to allow the children come to Him, not hindering them in any way. He manifested both masculine and feminine traits.

Twelve years ago, I had a dream and a vision in which I was shown the state of manhood in the world today. This vision was from God and it led me to become a men's pastor. In the dream, I saw God calling His sons back. In the dream, I asked God where all the men of God were. He said there were a lot out there, but they were separated into tribes. One tribe did not speak to the other tribe but God showed me He wanted to build a nation of sons. After that, I started my mission I received from God to unite the tribes.

I am currently the men's pastor at Sacred Exchange Fellowship where I oversee a ministry called Rally Point. Our objective is to awaken and equip men to be who they are called to be so they can come together as one family with God as their Father. We also encourage them to be the fathers, husbands, co-workers, and bosses we are all supposed to be as followers of Christ.

My heart's desire is to see the men of this world take back the ground we have lost because societal pressures have caused men to be either absorbed in work or to avoid their responsibilities. It's time to reclaim our daughters, sons, and families, but in order to do that, we must step away from the cultural view of manhood and walk into God's Kingdom view of manhood. This will require a transition from not only thinking with our heads but also feeling with and then following our hearts.

We as men are in a war against ourselves. Much of the battle is within us which is the reason any change must start and emanate from our inner being. We must put our faith in something greater than we are. We are meant to excel at whatever we are called to do, but before we can be effective in the world, we must learn to defeat the old man in us along with his old way of thinking.

Women seem to think that men do not like to talk as much as they do, but I have not found that to be true. Walk into a barbershop at the right time and you will hear more than you might want to hear. There men talk freely and openly with each other. If that's the case in that venue, then why is it difficult to speak about something to someone of the opposite sex? It's because many women require men to respond from a part of his being he is not used to or comfortable accessing: his feminine side. That's an aspect of our being we aren't comfortable relating to or responding from.

This is because we have been taught that to deal with feelings is not manly. Thus, we aren't used to or skilled at sharing our hearts. We feel vulnerable and weak when we let people see our inner being. This is not how God made us to respond or function. In the Kingdom of God, it's a strength when we allow others to see our heart. So, if I'm going to explain these emotions and feelings in a man, I have learned an effective way to do so. That's what I'm going to explain in the rest of this book.

MY HOBBY

I have a hobby and it's called BBQ. I love to cook it and I especially love to eat it. I have two smokers, a flat top grill and a propane grill. I have a *YouTube* channel called "Wes's Smokehouse BBQ" where I share my recipes and all my "trade secrets." On my channel I talk through the many things I cook, from brisket to smash burgers. I know if you're a man reading this, I now have your full and undivided attention.

There's nothing I can think of that speaks more directly and accurately about masculinity than BBQ. Therefore, through this book I will use the metaphor of the smoker and its process to explain my insight into manhood. You will go step by step with me as I share my BBQ techniques to show how similar it is to how manhood is produced. By the end of this book, you will have a clearer picture of a mature man in Christ.

All of us are going through the smoker, which simply means we're all in a life process that's meant to produce manhood. The problem is most men don't know they are in a process. Once you realize you are being molded and shaped into the man you are called to be, the process becomes a bit easier to endure and you can also cooperate with it more fully. At the end of each chapter, I have included some questions for you to further consider the material I have presented before you move on. These are ideal for individual or group study, so I hope you will take your time and perhaps even record comments in your journal. Here's a sample of what you can expect.

REFLECTION QUESTIONS

1. AS YOU LOOK BACK, HOW HAS GOD SHAPED YOUR LIFE?

2. WHAT LIFE SITUATIONS HAVE YOU GONE THROUGH THAT BROUGHT YOU TO THE PLACE YOU ARE TODAY?

3. CAN YOU SEE YOUR PROCESS MORE CLEARLY? IF SO, WHERE ARE YOU IN THE PROCESS AND WHERE DO YOU NEED TO GO?

Before you go on to the first chapter, think about the status of your manhood. Ask yourself some serious questions and answer them honestly. Am I the man God has designed me to be? How do I become the man God has called me to be?

**NOW LET'S GET INTO
THE PROCESS OF
WHAT IT MEANS TO GO
*THROUGH THE SMOKER.***

WESLEY PENNINGTON
COVENTRY, RHODE ISLAND
DECEMBER 2021

CHAPTER 1

THE
PREPARATION

"Give me six hours to chop down a tree and I will spend the first four sharpening the axe." – Abraham Lincoln

If you are in a time when God is preparing you for your future role and ministry, He's now determining if you need to be tenderized and what kind of seasoning will be required. This is the time of preparation *before* you're ready to go into the smoker. At this point, if the brisket could think, it would be wondering, "What will become of me?" Have you ever had that thought?

At this point, however, the brisket can't know what the end will look like—and the same will be true for you. You may have a general idea but only God can see the final result, just like only the chef or cook knows what the finished product will look and taste like. What's more, it's totally up to the chef as to what the brisket will become. In our lives, it's completely up to the Master Chef, the Lord Almighty, to determine what we shall be made into.

I remember when I was being prepared for the smoker. I was at a stage in my life where I didn't know what was going to happen from one day to the next. To make matters worse, I had no idea I was even in the process. I had no clue that there was an all-mighty God who cared for me and was actively engaged to transform me from what I was into what He intended. In fact, all my trust and belief were not in A*lmighty* God but rather in all-mighty me. I neither trusted anyone, nor would I seek or ask for help. I was the typical male, thinking I didn't need anyone or anything. The truth was, however, that I was lost, and God had started the process of transformation. Before I could be who I had been called to be, I had to be prepared for the smoker that I was about to enter.

When I get the meat ready for the smoker, whether it's a brisket or a pork butt, it must be prepared. The preparation is taking it from a frozen or packaged state to a ready state, which means getting the brisket ready for tenderizing. We will get to the tenderizing in a minute, which is also part of the preparation. However, first, I must get the meat ready, which requires that I thaw it if necessary and then clean it.

I must get all the packaging off and do away with the blood and messiness in which the meat may come. This gets the meat ready for the next step. When God is preparing us, we are going from a frozen state for some of us and a messy state for all of us to a state that He can use. We must be cleaned off and ready for the next phase. All our past hurts, past mistakes, past blunders, and our old perspective must be dealt with. This is a messy time and a bumpy journey.

Most of us would not want to eat the brisket if we saw it in its bloody, messy state. The good news, however, is that the chef knows what the brisket will become even when it's in this state. The experienced chef sees the brisket at its finished state from the beginning. Just the same, God sees us in our finished state even when we are in the bloody and messy state. When we are at our worst, God sees us at our best as we will be.

When I was in the place of preparation, I was feeling down and on the verge of quitting everything, including my faith. One day, I got up and went into the bathroom to brush my teeth. As I was brushing, I heard a voice say, "Why do you doubt yourself even though I never have?" I looked into the mirror and I knew who had spoken to me. As I stood there, I got chills all over my body. I knew I wasn't hearing things. I'm not claiming I heard an audible voice, but I heard the voice in my spirit, and it was not my voice. The voice of God spoke to me at the exact time I looked in the mirror.

So from that point on, I never doubted myself—or the fact that God was with me and working in me. I stopped second-guessing and started trusting God. God sees us as we are to be, not as we are. God sees us as we will be when we are in the messy, bloody, uncertain, beat-down, no-one-wants-to-see-us stage. God sees the warrior; He sees the beauty. When everyone else may close the door on you, when everyone else has turned away from you, God says, "I love you." In fact, that's the reason He's putting you through the smoker. However, before you can go into the smoker, you have to be prepared.

Preparation is one of if not the most important stages in the process of smoking the meat. Once you have cleaned and thawed the meat (brisket), it's then time for the tenderizing. It's critical to tenderize the brisket before we do anything further to it. The tenderizing breaks down the fibers of the meat, making it easy for the marinade and seasoning to get into the brisket. There are several ways to tenderize the brisket.

I have a meat tenderizer which is like a hammer with pointed, ridged ends at the tip. I use it to pound the brisket which is what breaks down the fibers of the meat. This allows the brisket to retain the water and hold on to the seasoning so it's rendered tender and moist at the end of the smoke. The other way I can tenderize it is to take a fork and puncture the brisket repeatedly, creating the same effect as the hammer. I can do the pounding or the puncturing and get the same results.

In the preparation stage, God tenderizes us when He shows us how much pain and damage we have caused in our lives and in the lives of those we love. As God prepares us, we receive insight concerning our past and present. God shows us what we look like in the eyes of our family and friends.

This is how God takes our heart of stone and turns it into a heart of flesh. He either hammers or pulverizes it in order to produce a soft heart instead of a hard one.

If you're like me and the revelation doesn't work at first, God uses a hammer. He comes in and smashes everything around us so we have no choice but to open our eyes. God tenderizes us so when He is done we are soft and tender to His ways as well as in our relationships with family and friends. This process continues throughout the cook, but it's the first necessary step for our transformation.

This is the process of becoming a man of God that we all go through who want Him to use us, some to a lesser or greater extent, others in different seasons of our lives. If you're reading this and realize that you're in the preparation stage of manhood, then thank the Lord. It isn't easy or fun but necessary for our development into authentic manhood. The success and depth of the process are contingent upon our relationship with God and our perseverance throughout the process. We cannot quit.

When I was going through the preparation stage, I was a mess—if I can be transparent with you. My word could not be trusted. I had no clue as to what real manhood was. I could offer excuses and say I did not have a good father figure in my life (and that is true). I could say I was confused and lost because of a worldly mindset, but all that will not hold water in the end—they are empty excuses. We can't point to or blame another for our lack of integrity or our wishy-washy manhood.

Thank God He opened my eyes and brought me through the smoker. Of course, I'm still in the smoker. We are all in the process of manhood until the day we meet Jesus face to face. More on that in the final chapter of this book. Through it all, my transformation has been directly connected to the strength and depth of my relationship with God.

I have been involved in men's ministry since 2009, and I have seen men fall away during the preparation part of the process because this is the part where things often get messy and stinky. As I stated, no one wants to see the brisket at the beginning because they will not want to eat it at the end. Therefore, I encourage you to hold on to God with all you have and by the grace He provides during this process. He is faithful and will bring you through it.

Don't quit or walk away because when you return, you will have to start all over again. How many of us have walked around the mountain too many times relearning the same old lessons again and again? Once the preparation is complete, it's on to the seasoning and the marinade. Let's examine that process in the next chapter.

REFLECTION VERSES

But the Lord said to Gideon, "There are still too many men. Take them down to the water, and I will thin them out for you there. If I say, 'This one shall go with you,' he shall go; but if I say, 'This one shall not go with you,' he shall not go" (Judges 7:4).

His breath is like a rushing torrent, rising up to the neck. He shakes the nations in the sieve of destruction; he places in the jaws of the peoples a bit that leads them astray (Isaiah 30:28).

"For I will give the command, and I will shake the people of Israel among all the nations as grain is shaken in a sieve, and not a pebble will reach the ground" (Amos 9:9).

"Simon, Simon, Satan has asked to sift all of you as wheat" (Luke 22:31).

REFLECTION QUESTIONS

1. HOW HAVE YOU BEEN SIFTED?

2. IS GOD PREPARING YOU, OR HOW HAS GOD PREPARED YOU, FOR YOUR SMOKER?

3. HAVE YOU BEEN THAWED OR ARE YOU STILL FROZEN?

If you are in the preparation phase, it's important that you hold on and remember you are not alone. This is a time of messiness and disorder. I would tell others during my preparation time, "If you pass by me and pick up an unpleasant odor, it's just my past mingling with my present process. It's my sin nature colliding with grace—but it will pass."

"When you have done all you can do to stand, stand" (Ephesians 6:13).

CHAPTER 2

THE SEASONING

"You are the salt that adds flavor to the earth, and the whole universe is waiting to savor your uniqueness."
– Michael Bassey Johnson, "Song of a Nature Lover"

Have you ever tasted a brisket or any type of meat that has not been seasoned properly? It's hard to eat and most of the time very tough to chew. God doesn't want men who are hard to handle and difficult to relate to. God wants men who are soft, compassionate, and tender to their wives and children and others they meet or with whom they interact. That leads to the next step in the smoking process.

The next step is to season the brisket which brings out its flavor. There are several types of seasoning a cook can use, and it varies from chef to chef as to what types of flavors they want to add. I have a YouTube channel called *Wes's Smokehouse BBQ* through which I share my BBQ techniques with anyone who wants either to learn how to smoke or just get some recipes. Just as a cook seasons the meat, God seasons us through our own experiences and life struggles that add flavor to us. We are all prepared by God's unique recipe for each one of us.

When it comes to seasoning a brisket, I use garlic salt, Lawry's All-Purpose Seasoning, and some salt and pepper. For my taste, this brings out the true flavor of the brisket and for me, the seasoning isn't to change the flavor of the brisket but instead to add and bring out its true flavors. What's more, I don't season right before I put the brisket in the smoker. The preparation and the seasoning usually takes place a few days before I put the brisket in the smoker. When God adds seasoning to us, it's to bring out the true flavor that we have residing deep down inside of us, which is there because He placed it there in the first place. Those will include our purpose, gifts, and creativity.

We may have to go through a time of seasoning before we're ready to go into the smoker. It depends on how much and what kind of flavor God wants to bring out of us, which in turn is dependent on the call He has for us. Therefore, be careful when you cry out and ask the Lord to use you in a powerful way. You may actually be asking for some additional seasoning. The point to remember, however, is that the seasoning used is always up to the chef, and to some extent, those who will consume it. Since God is doing the cooking and knows who will eventually "consume" the work He has done in your life, He usually puts the seasoning on liberally.

There's a common practice for seasoning the

brisket or any type of meat you're going to smoke. Before the cook applies the seasoning, they first have to apply a base. This is usually some kind of liquid like olive oil, mustard, butter, or whatever they prefer. This base goes on before the seasoning in order to hold the seasoning on to the brisket. If you didn't apply the base, the seasoning would fall off before you put it in the smoker. Usually the base doesn't add any flavor but simply serves as the binding agent for the seasoning.

In preparing someone for manhood, God also uses a base which holds the seasoning. The base could be your wife, your children, or your job, including your boss and your co-workers. God will use whatever He needs to get you moving in the right direction. This is the catalyst that allows the seasoning to flavor you so your life lessons will stick and develop your character, making you more sensitive, more compassionate, more forgiving. These are the flavors of God. When the man of God is seasoned properly, these flavors and odors emanate from him and all who are around him can detect his fragrance.

One of the seasonings that's regularly mentioned in the Bible is salt. Almost everyone uses it in cooking as I do when I season my brisket. Jesus had this to say about salt: "You are the salt of the earth. But if the salt loses its saltiness, how can it be made salty again? It is no longer good for anything, except to be thrown out and trampled underfoot" (Matthew 5:13). Jesus said that we men should be the salt of the earth. What did He mean?

In Jesus' day, salt was used not only to season food but also to preserve it. He was saying that we need to serve a positive purpose through our presence wherever God chooses to place us—family, work, church. We are to hold things together and preserve the good things God is doing in our lives and encourage the good things He is doing in the lives of others. What's more, we are to "taste good" throughout the process being kind and gentle but firm.

Later, the Apostle Paul instructed us, "Let your conversation be always full of grace, seasoned with salt, so that you may know how to answer everyone" (Colossians 4:6). Our speech is to be seasoned with salt so others will be thirsty to hear and learn more of what the Lord is doing in our lives and the lessons He is teaching us.

However, as men we are not to be salty. It was once said that when a sailor used vulgar language, he was described as "salty." James in his epistle wrote, "Can both fresh water and saltwater flow from the same spring?" (James 3:11). He was writing about our speech and was warning us not to be salty in our conversations while at the same time having some salt in our words that will serve as an incentive for others to hear and learn more of what we have to say about God and His work in our lives.

Before the heat is turned on, the seasoning, or as the grill masters call it, the rub must be applied. The seasoning is going to add to the flavor God wants to produce on the other side of the cook. I usually season my brisket at least two days before I do anything else. As stated earlier, the preparation and seasoning are probably the most important steps in the cook.

The seasoning process of manhood often puts us in good standing with God and man, although just like brisket, some may not prefer the recipe God used for the seasoning. Believers may encounter people who don't like them just because they are believers. You won't be able to please or reach everyone once you are seasoned and released to your God-given purpose. If you cooperate with the process, however, many people will be happy to see you come instead of happy to see you go. When you have the right disposition in life, you see things in a totally different way. That's the reason God seasons you, so your perspective will change until you have His view of things. You will start to experience and interpret your life differently than you previously did.

When you get seasoned, you start to see things from other people's perspective. You're less *self-centered* and more others-focused and God-centered. You are open to their pain and problems because you aren't totally consumed by yours. When you're seasoned properly and encounter someone who isn't, you will have compassion for them and extend yourself to them in a helpful, encouraging way.

With all this talk of compassion and being tender, don't think God will take away from you your toughness or manliness. God will restore these attributes later, but at the beginning of the process, God has a lot of heart and soul work to do in you. The pit master can't tenderize the meat after it is cooked. It must be done before they even start. Then later the bark of the meat will be developed through time and heat. However, I'm getting ahead of myself.

I can already taste the brisket when I'm preparing it. I can see, smell, and taste what it will become. In the same way, God can already see, smell, and taste what you are to become. That's why it's said that God sees you as you are to be, not for who you are right now. When you're done, you'll be a pleasing aroma unto God which we're clearly instructed to be:

> For we are to God the pleasing aroma of Christ among those who are being saved and those who are perishing (2 Corinthians 2:15).

> I have received full payment and have more than enough. I am amply supplied, now that I have received from Epaphroditus the gifts you sent. They are a fragrant offering, an acceptable sacrifice, pleasing to God (Philippians 4:18).

One of the techniques I use when I apply the seasoning is to put it on the brisket by hand, working it into the fiber of the meat. I do this so the seasoning (rub) really holds to the brisket and actually becomes a part of it. There are going to be some struggles you will have to go through. These struggles will feel like pressure is being applied to you and you are correct in that assessment for, in fact, the hand of God is actually applying the pressure, working His character into your being at its core.

He's pressing in the seasoning to become a part of you so when you go through the cook nothing falls off—in fact, it melts in and becomes part and parcel with your being and an important part of your flavor. Therefore, don't be afraid of the pressing. It's just God preparing you for the smoker. When an olive is being pressed, it's the only way to get the best parts of the olive out of it. The same is true for you, which is why God presses things out of you and then into you.

Some may differ with my smoke strategy and style, but I season and let the brisket stand for a few days, and then I marinate it the night before I actually smoke it. We will discuss the marinade in the next chapter. Let me say now that the marinade works with the seasoning, but it also adds something special to it.

If God is applying the seasoning to your life, it is something to celebrate, not dread or avoid. Even though it might sting or be sticky and uncomfortable, in the end it will bring out the best in you. In the end, it will aid the process of making you into the man you were called to be—a true son of God!

REFLECTION VERSES

We are hard pressed on every side, but
not crushed; perplexed, but not in despair
(2 Corinthians 4:8).

"Give, and it will be given to you. A good
measure, pressed down, shaken together
and running over, will be poured into
your lap. For with the measure you use, it
will be measured to you" (Luke 6:38).

REFLECTION QUESTIONS

1. THINK ABOUT A TIME IN YOUR LIFE WHEN YOU FELT THE PRESSING OF GOD. DESCRIBE WHAT THAT WAS LIKE.

2. HOW HAS YOUR LIFE BEEN SEASONED?

3. WHAT IS THE TYPE OF SEASONING GOD HAS USED MOST OFTEN IN YOUR LIFE? SERVICE? SUFFERING? FORGIVENESS?

4. HAS YOUR SEASONING CHANGED OVER THE YEARS AND ADDED FLAVOR TO YOU? DESCRIBE.

CHAPTER 3

THE MARINADE

As stated earlier, I always marinate the night before I plan to place the brisket in the smoker. Everyone does not choose to marinate a brisket, but I do. The brisket actually needs to marinate twice: before the cook and during the cook. The reason I marinate the brisket is twofold. First, it adds another layer of flavor to the brisket, and second it adds moisture to the brisket because it loses fluid as the temperature rises in the smoker.

Have you ever had a dry roast or a bite of dry brisket? It's like eating the sole of your shoe, which is the reason the marinade is so important. I use all different kinds depending on how I want to enhance the flavor. No matter the seasoning you put on it, dryness will detract from the taste of the meat and the experience of eating it. No one wants to spend *all* the time it takes to cook a brisket only to have it come out dry.

God works in the same way. He does not

want you to go through everything life brings only to have you turn out dry. When I say dry, I mean a man without passion, compassion, or mercy. This is a man without feeling who, even though his heart has been turned to flesh, is still unable to show his true feelings.

The marinade is the added element that keeps you filled with the moisture of life. This is important because if God does not add the marinade, you can easily become cynical and angry when difficult or painful things occur. You can conclude the process of achieving godly manhood is a waste of time. That is how we become dry. We even start to blame God when we should see some events as the consequences of our mistakes and unfortunate decisions.

This is the reason I'm taking the time to write this book: I've encountered many men who were dried out because of life. The seasoning and marinade did not take hold. The reason they were dried out was because they didn't understand they were going through the smoker. I know this because that's how I once was. I was going through life without direction or purpose, taking the hits, riding the ups and downs (and there were more downs than ups). I was on the verge of quitting any attempts to transform into the man God wanted me to be.

About the time I was considering giving up, a man of God came into my life who challenged me. He told me I was a son of God, which was the reason I was going through the process that every son has to go through to become a man. This perspective changed everything for me. Once my focus was off me, I was able to focus on God.

Then God put it on my heart to awaken other men just as I had been awakened. I'm writing to let you know that you are a son of God, and therefore what you're going through right now is all part of the process. Once you realize you're going through a process, it becomes easier to endure—for it has a purpose and an end. The marinade is part of the process that keeps you sensitive and discerning.

Even now as I write this book, my heart is overwhelmed for you because your time of awakening is upon you, which is why God led you to this book. God is going to quicken the same Spirit in you that He did in me. You may wonder if you must continue to stay in the smoker. I'm sorry to tell you that yes, you must. God does not coddle His sons. He knows when to apply the pressure and when to release it. I've been using the analogy of the smoker as an accurate way to compare it to God's ways of applying the necessary ingredients so you can be successful. The marinade is one of those ingredients.

In your life, your suffering marinates and flavors your heart during the struggle. It could be the loss of a relationship, a job you really loved, or anything we allow to get hold of our hearts. Remember when I told you about two sides of your being: the masculine and feminine? Your feminine side is often the marinade which God touches and releases.

This is usually the side we would rather not have to deal with, the side most men feel is the weaker aspect of who they are. Truth be told, this side can and will be our strongest and most effective side when God is done.

In my life, it was the loss of my mother and then the loss of my family. When I went through a divorce, I felt like I had failed. Perhaps you can relate to this. I was in pain because I thought I had failed my ex-wife, my daughter, and God. I actually had a twelve-year falling away from my faith because of it. I shut down my heart and would not let anyone get even remotely close to me emotionally. I would not even let God get intimate with me. I fell into a protection mode meant to shield me from additional hurt at all costs.

I'm so grateful that God is more patient than I am and stayed with me through that dark season. He waited for me to get over myself. I didn't realize it then, but God was involved in my life the whole time—even when I could not feel Him and did not want Him. He was applying the marinade but I was clueless as to what He was doing. I stewed and rested in my marinade for twelve years.

I informed you that I always marinate my brisket the night before. Once I smoked a moose and I marinated the moose for four days because the meat was so dense and thick, but it was quite tasty when I finished smoking it. The extra time and effort were worth it and created a special culinary memory. In the same way, God chooses how long you will be in the marinade, which depends on how thick your heart is. My heart was very thick and my head much thicker so I needed a long time in both the marinade and the smoker.

The marinade helps to keep the brisket moist and tender. In the same way the marinade of God keeps you compassionate and sensitive to those around you. No one likes a dry brisket and no one likes a man whose heart is stern, unmovable, or insensitive. Like I had to do with the moose by leaving it in marinade for a few extra days, God must do the same with us. Once the process was complete, that moose was one of the most tender and tasty pieces of meat I have ever consumed. God knows how to produce the same effect in your life as well.

I already stated that the marinade is applied twice—once at the beginning and once after the brisket has been in the smoker for a while. The first marinade is a cold application and the second time is during the heat of the smoke. I will describe this process in a later chapter when I discuss the wrap.

I hope at this point you can see how God brings a man through the smoker to facilitate the making of that man. I want to encourage you to allow the process to occur and to fully cooperate with it. There's a loss of manhood in society and it's reached epidemic proportions. If you look around, you see many broken families and lost sons and daughters. God is calling us back to our families, to our wives and children. Scripture says in Malachi 4:6 that God will turn the hearts of the fathers back to their children. I believe He is doing that now, but for a man to truly become who he is supposed to be, God places him in and then brings him through the smoker.

These first steps the preparation, including the seasoning and the marinade, are vital to the cook and to the transformation of the man. God is like a master chef in that He will not just jump into the cook without the proper preparation. God never makes a bad dish. His meals are always on time and very satisfying. I have shared with you part of my process of how God put me in the marinade for twelve years. Actually, He had me in the smoker for much longer, but as I look back on it, I can now see it more clearly and I'm grateful for and humbled by His work in me.

One of the things God has shown me is that what I learn I can't hold on to. I have to pass it along to the next brother. In the same way, I want to encourage you to pass on a copy of this book to another brother as a gift. It's time for all of us to work together to awaken our brothers so we can break out of our tribes and come together as God's army. There's an army of men out there who are asleep and once they are awakened, we will see change in this world.

Before we put the brisket in the smoker, we must decide what type of wood chips we will use to generate the smoke. Also, we need to preheat the smoker and get it ready to go. It doesn't matter the type of smoker you use, the process is the same. In the same way, it doesn't matter who you are; God uses the same process. God is creative in the ways He uses to make men and applies all kinds of methods, but the process is the same. In the next chapter, let's put the brisket in the smoker.

REFLECTION VERSE

"He will turn the hearts of the parents to their children, and the hearts of the children to their parents; or else I will come and strike the land with total destruction" (Malachi 4:6).

REFLECTION QUESTIONS

1. ARE YOU DRY OR MOIST? IS YOUR HEART SOFT OR HARD?

2. ARE YOU RESISTING GOD'S PROCESS? WAS THERE A TIME WHEN YOU DID? LOOKING BACK, CAN YOU SEE WHAT GOD WAS DOING? EXPLAIN.

3. WHAT CAN YOU DO TO REACH OTHER MEN AND ENLIST THEM IN GOD'S ARMY?

4. WHO DO YOU KNOW THAT COULD BENEFIT FROM A COPY OF THIS BOOK?

When God adds depth, He adds moisture to the man. I hope your time in the marinade is not long, but it's all up to the Master Chef. He will determine how long you need to be in the marinade. I want to encourage you to allow the marinade to soak to the deepest parts of your being. Then you will be sensitive and discerning just the way God wants you to be. Let's go! We are on our way into and through the smoker.

CHAPTER 4

THE SMOKE

In the heated room, he often felt the outlines of his body,
the borders between him and the external world, grow
disturbingly fuzzy. – Ryu Murakami

It's that time in the process of smoking a brisket to actually put it in the smoker. The cook has preheated the smoker and added the wood. They have prepared the brisket for the smoker. Now it's time for the first phase of the cook. We call this the smoke. Actual smoke is only a part of the cook, for I only add smoke for the first two to three hours. The smoke adds another layer of flavor and helps to create the bark for the brisket. It's at this stage that cooks must pay close attention to time because if they over-smoke the meat, then all someone will taste in the end is the smoke of the wood, and all the preparations will go to waste.

Here's the thing about smoke: It emanates from fire and heat. When the fibers in the meat are heated and open, the smoke can easily permeate the meat. In other words, the heat allows the smoke to flow. When God adds smoke to a man's life, He's adding some additional flavor. The smoke is added as God starts to turn up the heat. It's the time when everything He has done starts to come together. The smoke is applied in the secret place. When I put my brisket in the smoker, it's dark and hot in there. The sweating of the meat mixed with the seasoning, marinade, and smoke starts the process for which the pit master is ultimately working.

When God places a man in the heat of His smoker, the sweating starts to mingle with the seasoning, marinade, and smoke and in that transition we become a mess. The meat is no good to anyone at that point, and sometimes neither is the man. The pit master was waiting for this moment because this is when the flavors and juices start to mingle and combine, transforming the meat from what it was to what it will be. It's the same with us when the Master of pit masters places us in the smoker. This is when our messy past mixes with the anointing of our potential.

You could look at a person in this stage and think him a hypocrite, but really what is happening is he's being transformed. He's between stages where he knows who he should be but is facing the reality he isn't there yet. It's the messiness of his past mingling with the transformation of who he is becoming that makes him look undesirable and unusable. A dear pastor friend of mine once said, "Your past will follow you for a while." He meant the messiness of what you have been through is exposed even though you're in the process of transformation—just like the brisket in the smoker getting the added flavor of smoke.

When you examine the brisket, you would say it's a mess. It has no color and you would certainly not want to eat it. As I stated in the previous chapter, however, the pit master sees the brisket for what it will become and not for what it is. God also sees us for what we will become and not what we are. It's in this time that God does His best and longest lasting work. This is when all the tenderizing and seasoning come together to help us in this transformative and inescapable phase.

As I write this book, I have been a state trooper in the state of Rhode Island for twenty-seven years. There was a time in my career when I felt as though I was in the smoker. I also refer to it as my time of being on the back side of the desert. I had between fifteen and twenty years on the force and all my classmates I had graduated with from the academy were getting promotions. Not only that, but troopers who came on after me were getting promoted ahead of me. Can you understand where I am coming from?

I was stationed in a remote part of the state and I felt as if I was forgotten. I believed God had hardened the heart of the colonel of the state police when I realized that no matter what I did, whether it was saving someone's life or making the most arrests or writing the most tickets, it didn't matter. Every time I saw a promotional list come out, it pierced me like a sword through my heart when I did not see my name on it.

I was a mess at the time and God was putting me through the smoker. My messy past was mingling with my transformational present. My motivation as to why I performed my job duties had to change. Was I doing the job to please the colonel or to please God? I ultimately chose to do the job to please God. When I made that decision, things didn't change for me right away. I was still left on the backside of the desert for a few more years. However, during that time I was able to study for and work on my pastoral license. I took classes and studied my Bible. I still worked as hard as I could, but my focus had changed and the promotions that came out no longer cut me like a knife when I was left off the list.

The smoking part of the brisket is important because it adds layers of flavor to the meat. Pit masters have to make a decision as to how much smoke to add because if they add too much smoke, then the meat just tastes like smoke and nothing else. However, if they add just the right amount, when you bite into the brisket, you taste the marinade, the seasoning, and the smoke. It all comes through and the layers or variety of flavor are brilliant to the taste buds.

God does the same thing with us. As we start to feel the heat of the smoker and the juices start to mingle and combine with the smoke, there's an actual transformation that occurs. That's the reason I often use the smoking of a brisket as an analogy to preparation for manhood because we all are at a different phase of the smoke. God, the ultimate Pit

Master, is using His best recipe to make the man—
to make you!

What's amazing is that the pit master can use
whatever kind of wood he wants. I tend to use ap-
ple, cherry, hickory, pecan, and mesquite, but I've
used peach wood in the past along with several other varieties. This freedom to use different kinds of
wood allows pit masters to vary their flavors from
cook to cook. God also loves diversity and chooses
from a variety of means at His disposal to prepare
His servants, with each one having a unique flavor.

The smoke part of the cook is when the heat
is added and the smoke is infused for added flavor. Once the smoking session is over, however, it
comes down to nothing but heat. As I mentioned
earlier, I usually only smoke for the first two to
three hours depending on the size of the brisket.
After the smoke is done, it's just a matter of letting
the brisket reach the internal temperature any pit
master desires.

God adds flavor to our lives by allowing us to
stay in the heat for a while. As stated, I was passed
over for promotions and then there was a time
when there were no promotions, just spans of time
when I was out there on the backside of the desert
working while feeling forgotten. It's during times
like those that God sets us apart so He can get our
full attention and believe me, during that season
of my life, God had my full attention. He was the
focus of every thought and emotion that emanated
from me. He set me apart from the rest of the state
police officers.

I felt the heat of feeling forgotten and lost. The only one on whom I could lean was God. It's during times like these in a man's life that God makes Himself present and accessible. This all takes place in a dark place where no one can see, and it's just the man and his God. To be honest, it's actually a beautiful place to be.

After the smoke has ended, the brisket is in the dark with nothing but heat and time ahead of it. It's then that the flavors from the seasoning, the marinade, and the smoke come together to become a part of the brisket. The bark is being established and the brisket is starting to take on a wonderful, delectable color. The heat from the smoker hardens the skin on the outside of the brisket so the inside stays moist.

We have to go through some things in our lives to produce a bark. The bark is a hardened exterior which protects us while keeping our inside tender. Don't get me wrong when I say that the bark makes us hard. Have you ever eaten burnt ends? These are the tastiest parts of the brisket. They look almost uneatable but once you bite into one, you discover that it's moist and tasty. The bark God creates doesn't make you hard in the sense of not feeling anything and caring for nothing. The bark God makes is what allows men to be tender, compassionate, and caring while still maintaining their resolve to serve Him no matter how much heat or pressure they experience.

When we realize we are going through this along with other men all over the world who are also being brought through the smoker, we learn to have compassion because we can empathize with our brothers in similar circumstances. I have compassion for you as I write this because I know you are in the heat of the smoker right now—or you will be soon. I encourage you to endure the heat because on the other side you will be perfectly prepared in the way the quintessential Pit Master wants you to be. You will be understanding, compassionate, and tender to the people around you— the complete man drawing on your masculine and feminine side.

The exterior bark will make you hardened to the ways of the world and the things you used to do. No longer will those things tempt or sway you because you will have a hard bark exterior that will protect you from the things of your past and the things to come. At the same time, it will keep you compassionate, merciful, and loving on the inside. The bark will keep the world out but maintain the essence of what the Spirit is doing and producing in you. It's truly amazing how God orchestrates and oversees the formation of a man.

Don't think, however, that this is the end of the cook because once the brisket is heated to the required temperature, it's time for the wrap. Just when you thought you were through it all, you discover there's more to come as you will learn in the next chapter.

REFLECTION VERSES

"They will neither hunger nor thirst, nor will the desert heat or the sun beat down on them. He who has compassion on them will guide them and lead them beside springs of water" (Isaiah 49:10).

"I cared for you in the wilderness, in the land of burning heat" (Hosea 13:5).

Shadrach, Meshach and Abednego replied to him, "King Nebuchadnezzar, we do not need to defend ourselves before you in this matter. If we are thrown into the blazing furnace, the God we serve is able to deliver us from it, and he will deliver us from Your Majesty's hand. But even if he does not, we want you to know, Your Majesty, that we will not serve your gods or worship the image of gold you have set up."

Then Nebuchadnezzar was furious with Shadrach, Meshach and Abednego, and his attitude toward them changed. He ordered the furnace heated seven times hotter than usual and commanded some of the strongest soldiers in his army to tie up Shadrach, Meshach and Abednego and throw them into the blazing furnace. So these men, wearing their robes, trousers, turbans and other clothes, were bound and thrown into the blazing furnace. The king's command was so urgent and the furnace so hot that the flames of the fire killed the soldiers who took up Shadrach, Meshach and Abednego, and these three men, firmly tied, fell into the blazing furnace (Daniel 3:16-23).

Therefore, since we are surrounded by such a great cloud of witnesses, let us throw off everything that hinders and the sin that so easily entangles. And let us run with perseverance the race marked out for us, fixing our eyes on Jesus, the pioneer and perfecter of faith (Hebrews 12:1-2).

REFLECTION QUESTIONS

1. REFLECT ON YOUR LIFE AND TRY TO FIND THE TIMES WHEN YOU WERE IN THE HEAT OF THE SMOKER. WHAT DID GOD USE AS THE SMOKE IN YOUR LIFE? FOR ME IT WAS THE LONG HOURS ON THE ROAD ALL BY MYSELF AND A COLONEL WHOSE HEART WAS HARDENED WHEN IT CAME TO ME.

2. WHAT IS THE CONTRAST BETWEEN THE OUTER BARK OF THE WORLD AND THE BARK OF GOD'S MAN WHO HAS BEEN THROUGH THE SMOKER? HINT: THE WORLD MAKES YOU UNCARING AND NOT

COMPASSIONATE, WHILE
THE BARK OF GOD MAKES
YOU JUST THE OPPOSITE.
WHERE DOES YOUR BARK
COME FROM? GOD OR THE
WORLD?

3. WHAT CAN YOU LEARN
FROM THE STORY OF
THE THREE YOUNG MEN
IN DANIEL WHO WERE
THROWN INTO THE
FURNACE? HAVE YOU
HAD A FURNACE-LIKE
EXPERIENCE? DID YOU
FIND GOD IN THE FLAMES
WITH YOU?

Now take a deep breath, exhale, and let's
go on to the next chapter.

CHAPTER 5

THE
WRAP

God is completely sovereign. God is infinite in wisdom.
God is perfect in love. God in His love always wills
what is best for us. In His wisdom He always knows
what is best, and in His sovereignty, He has the power
to bring it about. – Jerry Bridges

The wrap is another crucial part of the cook. You could eat the brisket at this point because it has reached the required internal temperature, but you would find the brisket tough and hard to chew. Plus, the brisket could be a bit dry inside. The wrap allows the pit master to add back some moisture into the brisket. By doing this, the brisket becomes tender and moist, the brisket that we all know brisket can be—that is if you have ever had some really good brisket before. I'm referring to brisket that when you bite into it, the meat falls apart as the juices fill your mouth. This is what the wrap produces.

Pit masters use different methods to wrap their brisket. I like to use aluminum foil to wrap it, adding some kind of fruit juice in the wrap. First, I take the brisket and place it on the foil. Then I bend the foil in such a way that the liquid will not run off it. Once I pour the liquid in, I tightly wrap up the brisket in the foil and put it back in the smoker—back into the heat.

When I felt I was on the back side of the desert, it was as though I was done. I felt I was ready. I was no longer angry because I had been on a journey with God who had delivered me from myself. My ministry was moving ahead and I could actually see the end of the road when I would receive my ministerial license. I had reached my wrapping point. What is amazing about this is that at just the point when we are about to become dry, God adds moisture.

God gives us hope along with time to breathe, but then it's back into the smoker. That added preparation time causes us to become super tender and compassionate. Just when I thought it was over, back into the heat I went. God was not done with me yet. This time when I went in, God put the cover over me and that cover was God Himself. There was still some internal work that had to be done for God wasn't finished transforming me from the inside out.

My supervisor was starting to notice me. I heard talk about my hard work on the road. God actually had Pharoah (the colonel) travel past me several times when I was working so he could take notice of what I was doing. Isn't that like God to harden Pharoah's heart only then to make him take notice? Still, however, no promotions came my way; I was still on the back side of the desert. God was adding back some moisture so I would not be dried out. God gives us streams of refreshing when we are in the wilderness and that was what He was doing for me. I didn't realize it, but I was still in the smoker except that at that point, I was wrapped.

What the wrap does besides add moisture is to stop the bark from getting too hard, for by this time the color of the meat is where the pit master wants it to be. Thus, there's no need for more color, but there's still need for more heat. The wrap takes the brisket away from the direct heat but still allows the heat to enter the depths of the brisket. Have you ever been so cold that your insides feel cold? When that happens, the cold has broken through your outer flesh and is resting in your bones. If you are from New England, you understand what I'm talking about. This is the same principle of the wrap but with heat.

The heat has to get deep down inside the brisket. That's the reason the brisket must be wrapped at this point in the cook. The wrap allows the heat to get deep inside the brisket without causing the bark to get harder, making the brisket so tender that it falls apart in your mouth. God uses the wrap to continue the deep work He has begun within a man. The true transformation occurs during this time when you're back in the dark place again and it's just you and God. God wants to transform you from the inside out, which is why the wrap is so important to God and for us.

I thought I was ready, but God still had some work to do on the inside of me. It was during this time that I was even separated from the ministry God had given me. I told you that when the heat is being applied, there's a messiness created when everything comes together. That was me and I was still a mess. My past trailed behind me and at times caught up with me. I was actually placed on ministerial probation during which time I wasn't permitted to carry out any ministry activities. I was at a loss as to what to do, but this was when I clearly heard from God like at no other time of my preparation.

I was put on probation for six months and I found myself separated at my job and also at church. At the time, I did not realize this was part of the heat in the cooker or that there was more tenderizing that needed to happen in me. The Lord instructed me that during this time I was to serve and praise Him the same way I had always done.

The second thing God told me was to keep my eyes and ears open. I hated this process because I had no idea what was going to happen or how long it would last—or if it would ever end. I was holding on to God by my fingernails, but now that I look back on it, I see it was a time that transformed me. During that six-month period, I was closer to God than ever before. I was in the heat, but God was covering me and was with me. The third thing God told me was to inquire of Him before I did *anything*. I was on the backside of the desert on the job and in the church, but I was in a heavenly place with God.

The wrap is where the magic happens inside the brisket. It's when the tenderizing comes together with the flavor. The brisket is transformed from a tough, hard-to-cook piece of meat to a tender, beautiful work of art that everyone loves to consume—and even look at. I really enjoy this part of the cook. Sometimes I open up the smoker just so I can hear the juices boiling inside the wrap. I know when I hear it that things are coming together and my mouth starts to water, imagining that soon I will have a chance to taste it.

During my time in the wrap, I could feel the heat, but I could also see the light at the end of the tunnel. I knew God was doing a work in me because some real heart surgery was occurring in the dark place with just God and me. If you are reading this and you're in the dark place with God, I encourage you to take advantage of it by accessing God. Also, be willing to patiently wait. The brisket can do nothing other than cook when it's in the smoker. We can do nothing in the smoker other than let God have His way and be cooked. The time in the wrap when the heat of the smoker is doing its work is crucial to a successful brisket, just like it's crucial for us to be the men God has called us to be.

I usually wait until the brisket reaches around a 200-degree temperature before I take it out. That's when it's moist and tender and almost ready to be eaten. There's one more step, however, before we can have a taste. The importance of this step I have found is almost always underestimated. The last step in the cooking of a brisket is the rest period. In the next chapter, we will discuss what happens during that time.

REFLECTION VERSES

"But you, Israel, my servant, Jacob, whom I have chosen, you descendants of Abraham my friend" (Isaiah 41:8).

Then Moses cried out to the Lord, and the Lord showed him a piece of wood. He threw it into the water, and the water became fit to drink (Exodus 15:25).

REFLECTION QUESTIONS

1. HAVE YOU STARTED YOUR WRAP TIME YET? KEEP IN MIND THAT THE WRAP CAN LAST A WHILE.

2. ARE YOU READY FOR THE WRAP? KNOW THIS, WHEN YOU'RE IN THE WRAP IT'S JUST YOU AND GOD. WHAT A SPECIAL TIME IN A MAN'S LIFE THIS CAN BE.

3. WHAT AREAS OF LIFE DOES GOD STILL HAVE A WRAP OR A COVERING OVER YOU? WHAT DO YOU THINK HE'S TRYING TO ACCOMPLISH OR WORK OUT IN YOU?

CHAPTER 6

THE
REST

*"If there were no tribulation, there would be no rest; if
there were no winter, there would be no summer"*
— John Chrysostom

Part of wisdom is knowing your limitations and when you need to rest, and the pit master knows that the resting part of cooking a brisket is another important step. God is the ultimate Pit Master, and He knows how important the rest step is in the making of a man. Once you have wrapped the brisket and cooked it until it has reached a temperature of around $200°$, it's time for the rest. Most pit masters wrap the brisket in a towel or something similar and place the brisket in a cooler for a few hours. I usually leave it in the wrap and put it in the oven for at least three hours. If I can go longer I will, because the longer I rest it, the more the juices in the brisket have a chance to settle.

When the brisket is in the heat, those liquids are boiling and bubbling and moving around in the brisket. It's during the rest time that the liquids start to settle and cool down. If you cut the brisket too soon, all those liquids escape and are wasted. Also, if you leave it exposed without the wrap, the juices will escape and flow onto your dish or table, making a mess. By keeping it wrapped, the brisket stays in the juices that are trying to escape. What's more, the brisket can cool down slowly, helping to keep the juices in the right place—in the brisket where they belong.

In the same way, God places us in a rest period at times. It's during the rest time that we allow all that has happened within us to settle. The new way we are looking at and discerning the world around us will need to come together so we can understand how to use our new senses. It's during the rest time that we can look back and see what God has done. It's then that God gives us the ability to look back at our old selves so we can see how far we have come.

My rest was an amazing time with God and it's when God did the most remarkable things in my life. Think of the rest as the calm before the battle. The rest with God is that time between coming out of the smoker and your actual assignment in the Kingdom. When you're in the rest period, you feel as if you're ready to go but you're being held back. This isn't the doing of man but of God.

When I was on the backside of the desert and away from ministry, there's no doubt I was wrapped in the smoker like a brisket. After my suspension had ended and the great day came when I met with the elders of the church, I was a bit nervous because I had no idea what they were going to say. During the meeting, I was told that I went through the suspension like a champion. They were all proud of me and the way I handled the time away and I was reinstated as the youth director of our church. The heat was gone but the rest had started.

I was at the end of my study to be a minister and coming off suspension. I was ready to go but I had nowhere to go. I was praying and asking God which way I should go to get my license. I also knew that I was called to encourage men, yet I was still a youth director. I enjoyed being the youth director, and I suppose I had to start somewhere, even though I knew I was called to all men, young and old. I *sometimes* enjoyed those youth ministry days and if you have ever been a youth pastor or director, you know why I say *sometimes*.

What was great about my rest time was I had a chance to look back on my suspension and see and reflect on what God had done. I could see the times when I grew and the times when God carried me. Like I said in the previous chapter, during that time I heard powerful things from God—but He wasn't done. During the rest time, God ministers to us in different ways. His style then is not so rough or harsh, but tender and kind. In fact, God moved in a most significant way during my rest time.

Right after my suspension and reinstatement, I received a phone call from someone who had been a mentor and friend of mine. Bishop Gerald

Nelson called and reported that the Lord told him to give me a minister's license so he wanted to meet to talk about it. We set a time on Monday morning at 10 a.m. at a local breakfast place when I could hear what God had told him.

My daughter had just graduated from high school and was going to college in North Carolina. My wife and I decided to help her buy a car for her graduation. I had the pleasure of driving the car to North Carolina from Providence, Rhode Island. Let's just say it's a long, lonely drive when you're by yourself but for my daughter I was glad to do it.

My plan was to drive down to North Carolina on a Saturday night and arrive early Sunday morning. I would drop off the car to my daughter and then fly back home that day. Everything went well getting down to North Carolina. I had lunch with my daughter and was ready to fly back home with a feeling that my mission was accomplished. When I got to the airport, however, a storm came and settled over the area.

I went to the counter to get my seat assignment and was informed that my flight was delayed two hours. My gate had another plane parked at it and all its passengers were there waiting to board. An hour later, they boarded their plane, but we were directed to another gate to board my flight. I was glad because I would still be able to make my appointment with the Bishop.

I got on the flight and was getting comfortable when a flight attendant came on and said if I wasn't going to Albany, I had to get off the plane. I got off and went back to the ticket counter. By this time, more than two hours had passed since I had first arrived and I had to catch a connecting flight in Baltimore. The airline clerk looked and stated that the best he could do was to get me home by noon on Monday. I informed him that this was unacceptable because I had an important meeting to attend, and I had to get back home.

Then I noticed that the plane which was at my original gate was still there. The door was closed, and it looked like they were getting ready to push back. I asked the clerk where that flight was going and he said to Baltimore. I asked if there was any way I could get on that flight, figuring Baltimore was closer to home than being stuck in North Carolina.

The attendant typed in a few things and said he could put me on that flight, but I would most likely miss my connection in Baltimore. I decided to take the chance. They opened the door to the plane and I walked on. Everyone was looking at me, thinking the plane had been held up just for me—and it was. God held that plane at the gate so I could get on it. I got to my seat just in time for the pilot to say we were ready to push back from the gate and head to Baltimore. The problem was that I would get into Baltimore two hours past the departure time for my connecting flight.

The flight to Baltimore was without incident and I got off the plane and rushed to the nearest counter to ask the clerk from which gate the flight to Providence was leaving. She told me it was out of gate C-5 but that the flight had departed. I might be dating myself here, but do you remember the old O. J. Simpson commercials of him running through the airport? Well, that was me getting to C-5 for a flight that had already departed.

When I got to the gate, the plane was still there, but again all the doors were shut and there was a long line at the gate counter. I tried to get the clerk's attention to say, "Hey, I'm on that flight. Help!" but no one would look at me and some people in line told me to wait in line like everyone else. I had reached a dead end and did not know what to do. So, I prayed, "Lord, if You're with me, have the door of that plane open." I looked at the door and it opened.

One of the attendants came out for a final check. I ran and asked her if I could get on the plane, and she allowed me to get on a plane that was supposed to have already taken off. When I stepped on the plane, once again everyone was looking at me as if the plane was being held up for me—and it really was. It was held up for two hours and was not cleared to take off until I got on the plane. I did not get home until 2:00 a.m. Monday morning but I am glad to say I made my meeting with the Bishop. God held up both planes for more than two hours to get home for the meeting. This all happened during my rest time in God.

When God puts us in a season of rest, it's so He can restore us and make us into the sons He wants us to be. He does this for two reasons.

First, He does it to restore us to Himself. In fact, God's ultimate plan is to restore *all* of mankind to Himself. When we accept Jesus as our Savior, God starts the process of restoration which is why He puts us in and brings us through the smoker. He is restoring us to what we should be, or what we should have been.

Second, God restores us to us. My sister asked me one day how she could find herself. My answer seemed confusing to her but was actually quite simple. I said in order to find yourself you have to lose yourself. She asked what that meant. I responded in order to find your true self you must lose yourself in God. When we lose ourselves in God, we are actually on the way to finding our true selves because He is the only one who can correct what our sin nature has distorted. Another way of stating this is that Jesus is the only one who can make what is broken whole again. This is what I mean when I say He wants to restore us to us.

Going through the smoker is the process God uses to restore us to Himself and to us. The only way we can be any good to anyone else is if God makes us good with Himself first. After that, He restores us to who we are supposed to be. It's impossible to find yourself in a bottle or a pill. You can't find yourself in a drug or a relationship or a job. The only way to find who you are is through a relationship with Jesus Christ. Then when you find Him, He puts you through the smoker. This is why the rest period is such an important part of the smoking process because rest leads to restoration.

We're restored by God and become sons who are compassionate, caring, and forgiving as we pass through the smoking process.

The Bible has a lot to say about smoked meats if you pay attention. God is the master Pit Master, so He brings us through the smoker to make us into the children of God He has called us to be. Truth be told, we probably go through the smoker several times in our lives, being reheated and refreshed to be served again. Each time God brings us through the smoker, it's to bring us higher and take us deeper into who He is—and to ensure we fulfill our destiny.

I shared with you some of my life experiences to illustrate how God works. In the previous chapter, I filled you in on what God did in my work and spiritual life to show that He gives us rest in order to get us moving again. The preparation, the heat, the wrap, and the rest are all to get us moving in the right direction toward our destiny, the ultimate climax for our lives. We should all strive to reach the goal God has planned for us. It's time we start to live a life worthy of the One who created us, a life worthy of those who are called sons of God.

The rest of God is like being on a mountain top with Jesus, like Peter, James and John were when they were on the Mount of Transfiguration. Peter wanted to build shelters and stay there, but Jesus would not allow them to linger there, and we cannot stay on our mountain. The mountain is only to refresh us and give us rest. Then we must go back down to the valley where the work needs to be done. Just like for the brisket, the rest time must end so the time to eat can come.

One of my favorite parts of the smoke is when the rest is over and I open the brisket to take a look at it. The smells that fill the air are exhilarating for me. I know the brisket is done and I'm able to observe my work. The Lord feels the same way with us when He opens us after we have gone through the preparation process. The work of bringing us through the smoker is almost done and He gets to take the first look at what we have become. After that, we must live a life pleasing to God. The Bible calls it being a pleasing aroma to God. We will discuss what it means to be a pleasing aroma in a chapter to come.

REFLECTION VERSES

The priest is to splash the blood against the altar of the LORD at the entrance to the tent of meeting and burn the fat as an aroma pleasing to the Lord (Leviticus 17:6).

Present your burnt offerings on the altar of the LORD your God, both the meat and the blood. The blood of your sacrifices must be poured beside the altar of the Lord your God, but you may eat the meat (Deuteronomy 12:27).

REFLECTION QUESTIONS

1. HAVE YOU EVER HAD A TIME OUT OR BEEN PUT INTO A SEASON OF REST WITH GOD? WHAT WAS IT LIKE? WHAT DID GOD DO FOR AND IN YOU DURING THAT TIME?

2. WHEN I WAS IN MY REST TIME, I HAD TOTALLY GIVEN MY FUTURE, MINISTRY, JOB, AND REPUTATION TO THE LORD. WHAT AREAS OF YOUR LIFE DO YOU NEED TO FIND REST IN BY GIVING THEM OVER TO HIM?

3. GOD DELAYED TWO PLANES JUST SO I COULD GET ON THEM AND GET HOME FOR AN IMPORTANT MEETING. DESCRIBE A TIME WHEN GOD DID SOMETHING LIKE THAT FOR YOU. HOW DID IT MAKE YOU FEEL? WHAT DID YOU LEARN FROM IT?

God does a deep work in you that will produce lasting results. He will put you in places where you will serve and minister to others, but what you do is ultimately and mainly for Him. Yet at the same time, He will ask you to share what you have become with others. Keep that in mind as we move on to talk about being willing to share what you have learned with others to help them on their way.

CHAPTER 7

BRISKET
FOR ALL

If we have no peace, it is because we have forgotten that
we belong to each other. – Mother Teresa

Love only grows by sharing. You can only
have more for yourself by giving it away. – Brian Tracy

Whenever I prepare a brisket, I never make it just for myself. I always make enough to share with others. I once made a 17-pound brisket and after I finished it, I called my brother over and gave him half. Then I called some friends over to have a feast. Even someone's leftovers can help another person. It was brisket for all! We must learn to share what we have been given or we will lose it. God wants what He has created to be shared with all. That's what He did after the creation of the world. He created it and then shared it with mankind.

There's a spiritual concept that's foreign to our sin nature and that is if you give it away, you will eventually receive even more. This is a concept that to the world sounds crazy, but to God is the norm. How can someone have more when they give away what they have? When we share what God has given us, He always gives us more. It's like having a glass of water. If you drink it all, God comes and refills it for you, but if you hold on to it too long, the water will become stagnant and undrinkable.

One of the points I always stress to men at our Rally Point meetings is that what God gives you is not for you. God brings us through the smoker to share our experiences and knowledge with others. That's one of the reasons I'm writing this book. We must share what we have been given and the lessons learned from what we have gone through. This will help the next man as he goes through the smoker. I have shared with you my experiences and knowledge so you can then go through the smoker more easily and quickly than I did. After that, however, you must share what you have learned with the next man. This is how God replicates the process.

Think about it for a second. God sent His Son and since then, every person who has accepted Jesus as Savior is in the process of becoming like Him. Jesus said if you have seen me then you have seen the Father, which means that the Father has replicated Himself in Jesus and through the Spirit we are being replicated into the likeness of Christ.

We are all going through the smoker for one reason: to look and act like Him. The blood of

Jesus speaks a better word than that of Abel because Abel's blood cried out for revenge, but Jesus' blood cried out for forgiveness. Because of that, whenever God the Father looks down on us, He sees His Son because we are covered by the blood of Jesus. That is the reason the work of God must be shared with others.

I often think of when the Israelites were in the wilderness and God was feeding them fresh manna every day. If they tried to store it for the next day, it would spoil so they could only harvest what they could use for the day. As we are brought through the smoker, it's for the purpose of showing who God is to someone else and that's why we must be willing to share. I know this is a far cry from what the world says we need to do. The world says we should hide and keep secret what made us successful, but God says the one who will be the greatest is the one who serves others. In other words, we can't keep it a secret; we must be willing to share what God has given us and who He has made us to be.

When I share my brisket, I like to slice it thin and serve it as is. Then I put some BBQ sauce on the side for dipping. This is so the person receiving the brisket can taste the pure flavor of the meat, but if they want, they can then add some BBQ sauce. I once went to a famous steakhouse and I ordered a 24-ounce steak. When the steak came, I asked the waiter for some steak sauce. He looked at me, laughed, then said, "Take a bite, and when I come back, if you still want the steak sauce, I will get you some." I took his advice and the steak was so juicy, tender, and flavorful that I understood why he did not immediately bring the steak sauce. There was no need for it.

In the same way, when God brings us through the smoker and we are finished, there's no need for anything else to be added. When we are around other men, they will be able to smell, see, and hear the flavors flowing from within us. It's like being somewhere and smelling something so good that we can't wait to taste and eat it. It is the same with the men of God who have gone through the smoker. Others see, smell, and hear them and they want what they have so they can be like them. This gives us an opportunity to share what we have been given. Just like the cooked brisket is best shared, so we must share what God has done in us with others.

One of the most enjoyable things I have a chance to witness is when someone truly enjoys my food. This brings me great joy to know that someone is enjoying what I have created. Our God feels the same way when we share and others have a chance to partake in His goodness through us. This brings Him joy to see what He has created being shared and enjoyed. This is part of how we become a pleasing aroma unto God. When we allow our light to shine for others, we are giving God honor. We are glorifying the Master Pit Master, and we are expanding His Kingdom. Now it's time to talk about what a pleasing aroma you are.

REFLECTION VERSES

Jesus answered: "Don't you know me, Philip, even after I have been among you such a long time? Anyone who has seen me has seen the Father. How can you say, 'Show us the Father'?" (John 14:9).

You have come to God, the Judge of all, to the spirits of the righteous made perfect, to Jesus the mediator of a new covenant, and to the sprinkled blood that speaks a better word than the blood of Abel (Hebrews 12:23-24).

The Israelites ate manna forty years, until they came to a land that was settled; they ate manna until they reached the border of Canaan (Exodus 16:35).

"The greatest among you will be your servant" (Matthew 23:11).

REFLECTION QUESTIONS

1. DO YOU SHARE WHAT GOD HAS GIVEN YOU, OR DO YOU HOARD IT AND KEEP IT TO YOURSELF?

2. HOW CAN YOU MORE EFFECTIVELY SHARE WHO YOU ARE AND WHAT GOD HAS DONE AND IS DOING IN YOUR LIFE? GIVE TESTIMONIES? SMALL GROUP PARTICIPATION? SOCIAL MEDIA? SERVING IN THE CHURCH OR COMMUNITY? CAN YOU THINK OF OTHER WAYS?

3. CAN YOU THINK OF A TIME WHEN SOMEONE ELSE SHARED WHO THEY WERE OR WHAT THEY KNEW WITH YOU? WHAT DIFFERENCE DID IT MAKE IN YOUR LIFE?

It can be a difficult thing to overcome our love for privacy and our fear that we may be drawing too much attention to ourselves. But if God has done great things in and for you, you are to broadcast the good news far and wide. That's part of being a pleasing aroma to Him and others—although there are some who won't like the aroma of God coming from you. That's okay, for God can still use your aroma and testimony to touch and help bring them to Him.

CHAPTER 8

A PLEASING AROMA

*"But its entrails and its legs he shall wash with water.
And the priest shall burn all of it on the alter,
as a burnt offering, a food offering with a pleasing aroma
to the Lord" (Leviticus 1:9).*

Man has been sacrificing animals and burning them on altars since the beginning of time. Abel sacrificed his animal to the Lord, and it was a pleasing aroma unto God. One of the reasons I started getting into smoking meat was this thought that we could be a pleasing aroma unto God just like that meat. I pray every time I start to smoke something, "May this be a pleasing aroma unto You, Lord." As our smoked meats are pleasing aromas unto God, so may our lives be as well.

After God has brought us through the smoker and we have had time to rest, it's then time to live a life pleasing to God. When we live that kind of life, we are like the offering going up to heaven as a fragrant aroma. In 2 Corinthians 2:15, Paul wrote,

"For we are the aroma of Christ to God among those who are being saved and among those who are perishing."

It's just like someone who comes to my house after I have finished a brisket. The entire house is filled with the smell of the brisket. When we live a life pleasing to God, the heavens and our environment are filled with the pleasing smell. Just like I stick my chest out a little when I receive compliments for my food, God is smiling when He catches the scent of your aroma. He knows His work wasn't in vain.

Not only are we pleasing God, but we also enable Him to come and do some work in our families. Do you know that when the man of the house is saved and believes in Jesus, 90% of the time the entire house gets saved? God puts a lot of emphasis and importance on the man being a believer. That's why He puts us through the smoker and spends so much time preparing us, adding just the right amount of seasoning and marinade.

That's why He put us in the smoker with the perfect wood to add to the flavor. That's the reason He wraps us and allows us to rest so that by the time we're done, we're humble, compassionate, merciful, and forgiving—the image of His son Jesus Christ. Jesus was a pleasing aroma to His Father and in the same way we are a pleasing aroma when we are living a life God has planned for us and of which He approves.

Once I started to live a life pleasing to God, I went from the backside of the desert on my job to working at headquarters and speaking with members of the command staff every day. What's more, those promotions didn't pass me by any longer. I received two promotions and now the career God called me to as a trooper is a blessing to me.

As I write in 2021, I'm looking at a little more than a year before I retire and go into full-time ministry. I've been through the smoker and probably will have to go through it again before I meet my Savior. I can only hope I'm a pleasing aroma to my Lord. I want to encourage you also to be a pleasing aroma unto God. When we operate in the way the Chief Pit Master designed us to function, we become a pleasing aroma to Him, just like a brisket is a pleasing aroma to the pit master.

If we take a look at 1 Kings 18:30-40, we see an example of an offering on an ancient smoker. We also see how God responded to the man of God in this situation:

> Then Elijah said to all the people, "Come near to me." And all the people came near to him. And he repaired the altar of the Lord that had been thrown down. Elijah took twelve stones, according to the number of the tribes of the sons of Jacob, to whom the word of the Lord came, saying, "Israel shall be your name," and with the stones he built an altar in the name of the Lord. And he made a trench about the altar, as great as would contain two seahs of seed. And he put the wood in order and cut the bull in pieces and

laid it on the wood. And he said, "Fill four jars with water and pour it on the burnt offering and on the wood." And he said, "Do it a second time." And they did it a second time. And he said, "Do it a third time." And they did it a third time. And the water ran around the altar and filled the trench also with water.

And at the time of the offering of the oblation, Elijah the prophet came near and said, "O Lord, God of Abraham, Isaac, and Israel, let it be known this day that you are God in Israel, and that I am your servant, and that I have done all these things at your word. Answer me, O Lord, answer me, that this people may know that you, O Lord, are God, and that you have turned their hearts back." Then the fire of the Lord fell and consumed the burnt offering and the wood and the stones and the dust and licked up the water that was in the trench. And when all the people saw it, they fell on their faces and said, "The Lord, he is God; the Lord, he is God." And Elijah said to them, "Seize the prophets of Baal; let not one of them escape." And they seized them. And Elijah brought them down to the brook Kishon and slaughtered them there.

When the prayer went up, God sent His fire down to consume the sacrifice. This is a great example of what happens in a man's life after he has gone through the smoker. The consuming fire of God resides inside of him. When that happens, everything that's inside the man is consumed by God. He becomes a pleasing aroma to God, and when his prayers go up, God is sure to respond.

We have lost an important segment of society, which is men being true men of God. The good news is that God is calling us back to Himself. His Word says that in the last days He will call the fathers back to their sons. We're in the last days so therefore God is calling His sons, His fathers, back to their families. The way He's doing it is through the smoker.

There was once a generation of men who went off to war to protect their families. Today they are referred to as the greatest generation of all. God is calling another great generation of men to come forward and fight for their families. This army won't fight in a foreign country or land. This battle will be fought on their knees and the battles will take place in their spiritual war rooms. The question I have for you is: Are you a part of that army? Do you want to be a part?

I know I am and I do, and if you are or want to be, then you will have to go through the smoker. God bless you, my brother. I look forward to a time when we are all celebrating in the presence of our Lord and hear those words we all long to hear, "Well done, good and faithful servant."

If you're going through the smoker, know that you are not alone. The Lord has many sons who are ready to bear the heat with you. Keep in mind that God doesn't send you through the smoker; He's there in the smoker with you. He's forming you by His hand to be the perfect son you were created to be.

Thank you for reading this book and I hope it has encouraged and challenged you at the same time. Be the man God has called you to be for the world needs you. Your family needs you. The Church needs you. And now, let me share some final thoughts and then include some additional material about my ministry to men named Rally Point.

CONCLUDING THOUGHTS

When we started the Rally Point Men's Ministry, it was with the objective of changing the men in our church. Since then, however, the Lord has shown me that He's calling *all* His sons back to Him, not just those in our church. I once had a dream in which I asked the Lord where all the men of God were. He told me they are out there and there are many, but they are all in tribes. He went on to say that the tribes aren't talking to each other. Therefore, what was meant to be a nation of sons is a scattered remnant of men believing they are alone in the fight.

There are a lot of great men's ministries today, but no one ministry was ever meant to stand alone. Let's not forget that every men's ministry was given and created by God. It wouldn't make sense for Him to create a ministry that does not communicate and collaborate with the other ministries He created. We need the various ministries to work together in order to reach the masses of men, women, and children who desperately need the Lord. We must realize that we were not meant to congregate only in tribes. God's bringing us through the smoker so we can form a nation of sons doing His will here on earth.

During the Roman Germanic wars, the Romans had the upper hand because at the beginning of the war, all the German tribes were separated and didn't get along with one another. However, when one man united the tribes and formed a nation, it spelled the end for the Roman Empire as it was known. In the same way, the enemy has the upper hand right now because most of the men of God are in tribes and don't get along with each other.

There's a cry going out to all God's sons and all God's men's ministries to come together to end Satan's rule. His kingdom is about to come to an end. We must allow God to bring us through the smoker so we can be a part of that great army He's putting together. We must allow God to transform us into the men and sons we were intended to be.

As I consider the state of manhood, we have been found wanting. If we look at every situation in the world that has to do with the family, every problem comes back to a lack of manhood. There's a dearth of fathers in the land and that's because there's a lack of manhood. God's calling His sons back to our families, back to our children.

The question is whether or not we are willing to go through the smoker with God. It may feel as if we are going through the smoker alone, but we aren't alone. God's there with us, guiding us through the fire. When Nebuchadnezzar looked into the fire after he had thrown Shadrach, Meshach, and Abednego into it, he said, "I thought we threw three into the fire. So how come I see four and one looks like the Son of God?" (my paraphrase). You see, when we're going through the fire, God's right in the fire with us. Even though He's the one putting us in the fire, He's also the one preserving us and going through it with us.

Therefore, I ask you, my brother, to allow God to bring you through the smoker of life. Allow God to transform you into the man you are called to be. Your family needs you. Your children need you. The Church needs you. What's more, the world needs you to be the son you are called to be. Scripture says that the creation is eagerly waiting for the sons of God to be revealed. The creation is waiting for us.

When World War II started, many men went off to war to stop the evil in the world from spreading. People say that those men who were sent off to World War II were part of the greatest generation. I say that God is calling another great generation of men to come together again to fight the evil in this world.

However, this generation will not fight with bombs and guns. This generation will fight from their knees while praying for their families and their communities. It will fight with integrity and conviction, standing for their daughters and sons. My brother, in the end it all comes down to family. God wants to create a huge family and we're learning how to be in that family.

I know in my life I have been brought through the smoker and probably will have to go back in again because I don't believe God will be done perfecting me until I see Him face to face. The same is true for you. Let's go through the smoker together and allow God our Father to bring us through. The only way we can stand is together.

My prayer is that through this book you have a better understanding of one of the ways God develops His sons and daughters for the work He has called us to do. I pray that as you go through the smoker, you will be able to endure it, knowing God has sent you there and it's Jesus who is beside you. Be blessed, my brother, hold on, and fight because your salvation draws near. When you have done all you can do to stand, stand. Thank you for going through the smoker with me.

> Therefore, I urge you, brothers and sisters, in view of God's mercy, to offer your bodies as a living sacrifice, holy and pleasing to God—this is your true and proper worship. Do not conform to the pattern of this world but be transformed by the renewing of your mind. Then you will be able to test and approve what God's will is—His good, pleasing and perfect will (Romans 12:1-2).

Blessings to you!

REFLECTION VERSES

"You are to wash the internal organs and the legs with water, and the priest is to burn all of it on the altar. It is a burnt offering, a food offering, an aroma pleasing to the Lord" (Leviticus 1:9).

For we are to God the pleasing aroma of Christ among those who are being saved and those who are perishing (2 Corinthians 2:15).

1 Kings 18:30-40 – see chapter 8

"He will turn the hearts of the parents to their children, and the hearts of the children to their parents; or else I will come and strike the land with total destruction." (Malachi 4:6).

REFLECTION QUESTIONS

1. WHAT WILL DO YOU AS A RESULT OF READING THIS BOOK? WHAT CHANGES WILL YOU MAKE?

2. ARE YOU WILLING TO BE A RECRUIT IN GOD'S ARMY? DON'T ANSWER TOO QUICKLY. WHAT ARE THE IMPLICATIONS FOR BEING GOD'S SOLDIER FOR YOU AND YOUR FAMILY?

3. WHAT TRIBE(S) ARE YOU A MEMBER OF? WHAT CAN YOU DO TO BRING YOUR TRIBE INTO CLOSER RELATIONSHIP WITH OTHER TRIBES?

Again, thank you and bless you, and may your journey through the smoker be enriching, fulfilling, and life-changing. Once you are transformed, then go out and change the world.

This is why it is said "Wake up, sleeper, rise from the dead, and Christ will shine on you" (Ephesians 5:14).

MORE ON RALLY POINT MEN'S MINISTRIES

I thought I would share more information here about my men's ministry called Rally Point. You can find this information on my website, but since you have come with me this far in the book, I thought I would also include it here for you to read. I'm looking forward to doing even more with Rally Point once I retire from the force, but until then, I am actively involved in equipping men for the smoker. You can contact me for even more information or to start a Rally Point ministry in your area. I would be glad to come visit to get things started.

PURPOSE

The purpose of Rally Point is to stir the hearts of men back toward God so they can take their rightful seat at God's table. We also strive to turn their hearts back to their children, wives, and churches, to be the men of God He desires and can use! This is the reason the Bible says, "Awake, sleeper, and arise from the dead, and Christ will shine on you" (Ephesians 5:14).

MISSION STATEMENT

Our mission is to encourage men to be who God called them to be so they can walk in their purpose and fulfill their destiny. That will enable them to be the fathers, husbands, brothers, friends, co-workers, bosses, and owners they were called to be. We empower them to be courageous as they walk into their destiny.

RALLY POINT SERVICES

Rally Point offers a number of services and programs designed to emulate a wholistic approach to what it means to be a man of God in the church, your profession, and in your personal life. This includes but is not limited to:

- **Rally Point Men's Ministries:** A call for all men to come to the table of God. This is not a small group but a way of life—to walk with Jesus! Our objective is to build into men the integrity God requires.

- **Rally Point Consulting:** Special training and public speaking focusing on encouraging men through such topics as relationship building, diversity, and diversity training for businesses, individuals, and law enforcement.

- **Wes's Smokehouse BBQ:** Mixing purpose with passion, these video tutorials provide a variety of smoked meat recipes, grill equipment training, and more.

THE EIGHT VIRTUES OF RALLY POINT MEN'S MINISTRIES

At Rally Point Men's Ministries, we work to create the curriculum, tools, support, and fellowship necessary to continue building the integrity of God in men!

We have found that by implementing certain attitudes—or as we call them, virtues—causes a transformation to occur inside a man. Jesus' plan is to transform us from the inside out to form character in us as men and develop integrity from which we can then evangelize other men. Here are the eight Rally Point Men's Virtues we strive to teach and impart:

1. **Humility** is not thinking less of yourself but thinking of yourself less.

2. **Compassion** is thinking of others, understanding that you have fallen short so we are able to stand with those who fall short.

3. **Meekness** is control and discipline

under pressure similar to how war horses allow themselves to be under the control of their rider, putting all their strength at their rider's disposal and direction.

4. **Passion** is directing your feelings to the right place and having a passionate love for God your Father.

5. **Mercy** is forgiving others because you have been forgiven.

6. **Purity** is keeping your heart and mind on the things of God as well as keeping your mind and thoughts pure before God.

7. **Diplomacy** is keeping the peace by being a peacemaker.

8. **Courage** is standing up for your faith and what you believe in. Courage does not mean absence of fear but acting correctly in the midst of fear.

BONUS RECIPE

My recipes are available in my cookbook which you can download from my website. As an added bonus, here's a page from my cookbook with one of my delicious recipes.

INGREDIENTS

- 1 10lb brisket
- ½ cup olive oil
- ½ cup seasoning salt
- ½ cup orange juice
- ¼ cup brown sugar
- ¼ cup butter

- Pecan wood chips
- Aluminum foil
- Meat probe or thermometer

NOTES

Make sure your brisket is thawed completely before you begin. My preferred seasoning salt is Lawrys. When it comes to the right amount of pecan chips to use, everyone's smoker burns differently. Use as much as you need to fill your tray. Parchment paper can replace foil.

WATCH

Want to follow along with a video tutorial? Visit the YouTube link below!

https://youtu.be/g0Y9Bd4qT9Q

DIRECTIONS

Rub brisket with olive oil on both sides. Next, use seasoning salt generously on both sides. Pack in that flavor! Let sit for a minimum of two hours *(overnight if possible)*.

Preheat smoker to 275 degrees. Add in pecan wood chips. Place meat probe in brisket. Place brisket in smoker and let cook until a temperature of 165 degrees internal temperature *(about 2-3 hours)*.

Take brisket out of the smoker and wrap in foil. In wrap, cut butter into four sections and place on brisket. Add orange juice and brown sugar. Close wrap tightly and place meat probe back in brisket. Place brisket back into smoker until it reaches an internal temperature of 200 degrees. Remove brisket from smoker and let rest a minimum of 3 hours. Cut and serve with your choice of BBQ sauce.

MORE ABOUT
THE AUTHOR,
WESLEY PENNINGTON

Wesley Pennington grew up in Cranston, Rhode Island in a family of five boys and one girl, in which he is the youngest. He graduated from Cranston High School East and went on to study sociology at Western Connecticut State University. Wesley then became a member of the United States Army. He served a tour in Korea and upon coming back from Korea, he was assigned to the prestigious 82nd Airborne Division. During his time with the 82nd, Wesley was in one of the first groups sent to Operation Desert Storm.

Upon completion of his military commitment, he returned to Rhode Island where he worked for the West Warwick Police Department. After two-and-a-half years, he left there and went to work with the Rhode Island State Police where he has been employed since 1994. As coach of North Smithfield High School, Wesley's team won the 2019 State Championship and he received the 2019 Football Coach of the Year award. He currently serves as the football coach at West Warwick High School. He is also an ordained pastor. Wesley is married to his wife, Marissa, and has two daughters, Ashley and Eliana.

YOU CAN FIND WES'S YOUTUBE CHANNEL AT

www.youtube.com/c/Wes'sManStuff

ON FACEBOOK

Facebook.com/RPmensministry

ON INSTAGRAM

https://www.instagram.com/p/CUuWhLsrQWu/

ON LINKEDIN

Linkedin.com/in/Wesley-pennington-8575a13a/

CONTACT HIM DIRECTLY THROUGH HIS WEBSITE

www.rallypointmensministries.org

OR BY EMAIL

wesley@rallypointconsultingllc.com